THIS IS THE
DESCENT

THIS IS THE DESCENT

Rebecca Gunn

*To my nana and my grandpa,
who knew i could accomplish
my dreams.*

Table of Contents

NOVEMBER:

ONLY LOSING MONEY HERE, HONEY
GIRLS BEING GIRLS
FREEDOM TO BE
18 AS TOLD BY REBECCA PART ?
CAN YOU HEAR ME?
IS YOUR BRAIN ON FIRE TOO?
IT'S MY LIFE
18 AS TOLD BY REBECCA PART ?

DECEMBER:

18 AS TOLD BY REBECCA PART ?
PHYSICAL ILLNESS MEETING METAPHORICAL
    SILENCE
WINTER CLEANING
THIS IS THE DESCENT
DO YOU HAVE A CHAPSTICK I COULD
    BORROW?
DIFFERENT PERSPECTIVE
HOME REMEDIES
RE #57
THE GIRL YOU HAD BEFORE IS GONE
I HOPE YOU ROT
THE OTHER
45 MINUTES IN THE SHOWER OKAY
I'M STAYING STILL
18 AS TOLD BY REBECCA PART ?
TRAPPINGS
WEIGHTLESS AND HEAVY BUT CAN YOU
    HEAR ME
LITTLE GREEN COLOR ME IN ENVY
THIS IS TIME PASSING SLOWLY, QUICKLY,
    PASSING
SAD/MAD SAME THING NO?
SHE DOESN'T EVEN HAVE A SUICIDE NOTE

JANUARY:

YOU HONESTLY MAKE ME PUKE
THIS COMPANY SUCKS
DEATH IS TALKING TO ME
18 AS TOLD BY REBECCA PART ?
I AM FIGHTING A WAR IN ME
THE FIRST TIME IN THE ABYSS WAS VERY
    UNPLEASANT TO BE HONEST
CASSY!!!!!
PYROMANIACS DEATH
DO YOU HAVE A PLACE FOR ME TO STAY?
I'D LIKE TO SPEAK TO A DOCTOR
I'M SORRY, I'M SORRY, I'M REALLY TRULY
    SORRY
YOU'RE WORKING OVERTIME, RELAX
PLEASE TELL ME YOU FEEL LIKE I DO
MY INSIDES ARE TOUCHING MY OUTSIDES ON
    THE WRONG SIDE
A GIRL ISN'T A GUN, BUT SHE'S GOT A GUN
THIS IS YOUR CAPTAIN SPEAKING
18 AS TOLD BY REBECCA PART ?
NO CAFFEINE JUST ELECTRICITY
NO WAY, YOU'RE JUST HAPPY
MECHANICAL ENGINEERING
I THINK I'M DRIVING ME INSANE
MY TEETH KEEP FALLING OUT
EVERYONE AND THING IS LAUGHING AT ME
THE MADNESS IS OVER TAKING ME
ALWAYS A DOLL, NEVER A REAL LIFE GIRL

FEBRUARY:

YOU'RE UNFORGETTABLE BUT I'LL SPEND THE
   REST OF MY LIFE TRYING TO FORGET YOU
18 AS TOLD BY REBECCA PART ?
THIS TIME A GIRL IS NOT A GUN, BUT SHE'S GOT
   ONE AND THIS TIME SHES THINKING OF YOU
I KEEP BREAKING THINGS AND I DON'T FEEL
   ANY BETTER
18 AS TOLD BY REBECCA PART ?
I CAN'T GET RID OF THE BITTERNESS
SORRY FOR TAKING YOU FOR GRANTED
THE INTERTWINING OF ME
TIME IS CONSTANT AND ALWAYS THERE
TWO THINGS AT ONCE
DO YOU THINK I'M PRETTY?
18 AS TOLD BY REBECCA PART ?
ASLEEP OR AWAKE LIFE IS A NIGHTMARE
18 AS TOLD BY REBECCA PART ?
TWO WRONGS EQUAL SELF PRESERVATION
DON'T LET ME BE ALONE IN THIS MISERY
HOW DID YOU END UP IN MY BED?
LET ME DRIVE THE HIGH SPEED TRAIN
18 AS TOLD BY REBECCA PART ?
I'LL PLAY A DANGEROUS GAME, I'VE GOT
NOTHING TO LOSE
YOU SEE I HAD A RUN IN WITH A MIRROR
YES, YOU ARE IN FACT GOING CRAZY
IT'S DEPRESSION I'M NOT LAZY
COIN TOSS
VITRIOL POURING OUT
A GIRL IS NOT THE GUN, A GIRL IS THE BULLET
GOODBYE GOODBYE

MARCH:

I THINK YOU'RE A SCUMBAG
ENVY IN THE MORNING
DON'T WAKE ME UP
18 AS TOLD BY REBECCA PART ?
MY BRAIN IS ACCESSING THAT OTHER PERCENT
   THAT'S NEVER USED
THE REAL TRUTH ABOUT INNOCENCE
18 AS TOLD BY REBECCA PART ?
I'VE JOINED THE CIRCUS BUT I'M NOT HAVING A
   GOOD TIME
I DON'T REALLY THINK YOU'RE SEEING ME
DREAMLAND DOESN'T WITH THE WAKING
THIS IS THE CRASH LANDING
18 AS TOLD BY REBECCA PART ?
CRASH CRASH PUTTER PUTTER
IF OTHER PEOPLE DON'T NEED A BRAIN
   NEITHER DO I
IT'S NOT MY BIRTHDAY CAN I CRY ANYWAY?
YOU'RE THE WORST THING THAT EVER
   HAPPENED TO ME
YOU KNOW WHAT I MEAN RIGHT?
EVERYTHING IS BREAKING INCLUDING ME

THE ICEBURG

when i was   18
   i took a vacation to the   psych   ward
i got to not go to school for 10
                              whole days
while i was there,
               we talked about the iceberg
in this iceberg the tip is   anger
            the rest of the iceberg is   sadness
they teach you that you can't have   one
                              without the other
   rather   anger   is just a mask emotion of
                              sadness
i knew i was   sad   (severely they told me)
i however had just started being   angry
      what they didn't tell me was that
               i would spend the rest of my
                                        life

            going   up
                  and
                  down
this iceberg.
that when my brain didn't want to be
                              sad
it would turn to   anger   that would have me ready   to
burn   the   world to the ground.
   i had found this lesson riveting at the time.
now
      it   haunts   me every time i'm   sad
                  and every time i'm   angry.

THIS IS THE
DESCENT

September

18 AS TOLD BY REBECCA

when you're 18 (the day of) you do everything an 18 year old
can do. you go and get a tattoo behind your ear, you hit the
vape store to buy nicotine legally, and lastly you pierce your
nose. you are feeling the best you've ever felt. 18 is your year,
it's in your bones. when you're 18 you come home from these
excursions and your mother just shakes her head and you
tell her, i'm 18! you said when i was 18! she just sighs and
says i know. when you're 18 you throw a party at your house.
everyone comes and you play ping pong, beer pong, laugh
on the couch, take lots of pictures. you're very happy to be
surrounded by all your friends. when you're 18 you feel this is
the year things turn around.

WHO I AM

who i am is no concern of yours
bright and confident
glowing walking by you
words spoke with such conviction it must be true
ready for a good time
hesitant on said good time
dressed and ready to take on the world
yet lazy in the morning
an actress in the theatre
a retired soccer player
a girl with a broken heart who cried for months
daughter of parents who are now divorced
sister to two siblings each she is estranged from
living in a big house just her and momma
soon to be her, momma, momma's best friend, and son
who i am is of no concern to you
deeply sad yet happy to be here
desperate to feel love
lonely as if nothing is ever mine to keep
walking side by side friends feeling thankful and full yet
alienated by being darker than white
bravado in place of confidence
that fake it till you make it
that smile every one is looking at she learned from daddy
that pose in pictures (leg out hand on hip) engraved into her
from sissy
and that resentment building from brother
yes who i am is of no concern to you

i contain multitudes
my very own paradox
two things existing at once
you don't worry about me
but one day i'll want you too
for now who i am is no concern to you

18 AS TOLD BY REBECCA PART ?

when you're 18, one of your best friends throws a party to kick off the school year. you get there and it's tame. nothing too crazy. you start drinking and having a good time. then your ex boyfriend shows up. he says hello to you and you say hi and you hug. see, the thing is when you're 18 you have the same friends as your ex boyfriend even if you are at different schools. when you're 18 you're finally over the break up that happened the beginning of junior year and you are ready to start senior year. this party is doing it right. all year you vowed to party, pass, and graduate. you toured colleges over the summer and you are feeling good. the drinks are flowing through your veins. you feel it in your head. when you're 18, your ex boyfriend will be all over you at this party. people will ask if you guys are getting back together. when you're 18, you'll laugh and say, no, i deserve better. you do, and you know it. you just love the attention. it will go on like this for the rest of the night. you'll feel happy and light. a good start to the year you think as you get into bed that night. when you're 18, all you can think about is how things are finally looking up.

I HAVE FIVE TALLIES, HOW MANY DO YOU HAVE?

second big party of the year
right after the other
a birthday celebration
teenagers all around
drinks in hand
tallies on hand
buzzing around saying hello
falling on grass
drunk and happy
can't keep limbs straight
feeling on top of the world
with alcohol pumping through
the veins
it's a new year
a new age
so much to be seen

SENIOR SUNRISE

the sun rising
　　　donuts being passed out and ate
　　　　　　everyone in crowns they decorated
pictures being taken
　　　being blinded by the morning sun
oh! is this my good angle?

　　　the whole class sitting still for one picture
laughter　ringing　out
bittersweet　times
the beginning of the end

DO YOU ONLY FEEL HAPPY
WHEN INDUCED WITH ALCOHOL
AND A CIGARETTE DANGLING FROM
YOUR LIPS?

sometimes i find myself at the right end of a cigarette
after the drinks have been ingested my body moves more
freely
i go searching for a cigarette just to help the feeling sink in
that i'm floating
maybe to clear out the taste of the drinks i've drunk oh! i'm
drunk
it tastes so much better drunk than sober
oh! happy day! i think
everything is complete
i am complete
then i go about drinking and dancing and talking to my heart's
content with the right end of the cigarette towards me

GOT TO MAKE IT COUNT

last first day-
night before
me and kathy
picking out outfits
                    it's a big deal
                            it's going to seal the deal
set the tone for the year
excitement buzzing all around
this   no   this
           how   about   that
purple pants
           black top
i hate to be uncomfortable while i   suffer
ya know?
flowy purple pants
               v neck black shirt
always a v neck
accentuate the boobs
                    in the push up bra
yes, yes this will do
sandals to match
the black strap ones
and   done

CASSY, I'LL ALWAYS LOVE YOU

first day theatre class
and i'm getting a note
from the lovely cassy
a tradition of sorts
where she writes the lyrics
to songs
i've of course heard
and hands them to me
says happy senior year
i'm going to miss you

YOU CALLED I ANSWERED NOW WE ARE ALL IN MY BED

late night
receiving drunk calls
from friends
who are too intoxicated to go home
so they sleep at yours
in your king size bed
you and three other people
squished together
girl girl boy boy
so that they don't have to face their parents
and explain that they got carried away
swept up in the swing of things
it's a memorable night
like the cinnamon rolls in the morning you eat

SKATEEESKATEEESKATEEE

the girls doing anything for the boys' attention
like going to the skate park
getting on the board
and skating around
giving up and just watching
recording everything
making noise into the night

A MOMENT IN TIME

on top of the world

the girls the boys

surrounding

love from all around

deep belly snorting laughter

peace bliss

freeze this moment

this moment right here

with everyone on the couch

huddled around

people on the floor

freeze this moment

don't ever forget it

October

A GLIMPSE INTO THE LIFE OF TEENAGE GIRLS

seven girls packed in a bedroom
laying on the bed
talking this and that
playing music
strobe lights on
together hypothesizing
does he like me i think but maybe not
i was thinking of wearing this on monday
dazed by friendship and closeness
seven girls lay on a king size bed in a bedroom
soaking each other in
telling each other they will be friends forever

18 AS TOLD BY REBECCA PART ?

when you're 18 and in high school you have a lot of friends. somehow you all end up at the skate park. of course this is because of the boys. when you're 18, vlogging is super in. you're there with your phone videoing everything that goes on. asking questions, taking videos of your friends skating. when you're 18, this feels like a peak. nothing is bad when you're surrounded by friends having a good time. you guys are at the skate park at least four times a week. it's getting cold. you're in layers and layers. one time at the skate park you decide to try to go down one of the things. there's a name but you don't know it. when you're 18 and you build up the courage to go down it you fall off the skateboard. everyone claps though. they are proud of you. you are proud of you. feeling on top of the world. when you're 18 and you're at the skate park until the lights get turned off, you end up staring at the stars you can see. you live in a city so the light pollution is abysmal. you stayed there with one other friend. a friend you hadn't spent a long time with before and you guys talk. you're 18 and the stars are out, you're having conversation and you feel good. you would even call it euphoric. when you're 18, you feel like the world is at your fingertips.

YOU'RE CAUSING MAYHEM AT THE CAFE

nights like this
when the air is crisp
we are all huddled together around the table
smoking hookah outside the cafe
asking who can run faster
causing mayhem for the waiter
ignorance on the faces of teenagers
running through the parking lot
to test who can run fastest
the girls saying on your mark go
joy filled faces seeing the boys run like the olympics

GETTING HIGH IN THE BATHROOM AT THE MALL

homecoming
getting high in the bathroom at dinner
not thinking the pen was working
taking hit after hit
then starting to feel sick
sitting at the dinner table
woozy sleepy sickly
taking the stairs back to the
party bus slowly not all at once
inebriated arms are tracking
eyes not moving
arriving to the party house
drinking alcohol to balance the high
finding the sweet spot
feeling back to normal
if not slightly tilted

JUST A LITTLE GAME OF SUCK AND BLOW

just an innocent game of
suck and blow
amongst friends
kissing kissing
dropping it on purpose
kissing kissing
some longer than others
excuses to finally kiss
feeling jittery in a good way
heart beating fast
feeling on top of the world
this is the moment
you feel it in your bones
where you are supposed to be
kissing kissing

18 AS TOLD BY REBECCA PART ?

when you're 18 you decide it's time you start having more sex. you don't want someone new, your ex boyfriend will do. you snapchat him and tell him what you're thinking. he agrees rather easily. you set up a date you are both free. when he comes over that day you have sex. probably the quickest sex and it definitely wasn't anything special. when you go to the bathroom to pee and you wipe you see blood. you start to panic just a little bit. you go back to your room and look at your sheet and see smears of blood. when you're 18, you look at your ex boyfriend bewildered. you stare at him till he asks why you're looking at him like that. when you're 18, you tell him, *i know we have had sex before, but i think this time you popped my cherry.* when you're 18, he just laughs and goes to the bathroom. you sit on the edge of your bed and contemplate this event.

GET IN I HAVE SOMETHING TO TELL YOU

early mornings when the sun is barely rising
crammed into the red jetta
The heat blowing
windows up the gossip is too hot
no one can hear
getting ready for the hours ahead
deciding to skip or be late
never on time
the joys of senior year at your fingertips

18 AS TOLD BY REBECCA PART ?

when you're 18, you're in the lowest math class there is for seniors. thank god for that. math hasn't been your strong suit in years. you have three of your favorite girls in the class with you and you know you'll never get anything done. when you're 18 and it's a pilot math class all on the computer, you stare at the screen in misery and you turn around and whisper to your friends. senior year is gonna be pretty alright if this is the start to your day everyday.

THE HALLOWEEN OF THE DEVIL AND VAMPIRE

vampire-
          here to suck your blood
devil-
      here to take you to hell
one too many drinks   down the hatch
          arriving to the sink
to spew out the guts   of the devil
while the vampire watches   trying to be soothing
             but failing miserably
soon to be laying the devil in bed
saying get me if you need something
bowl to side
to catch the wandering

November

ONLY LOSING MONEY HERE, HONEY

kt has turned 18
to celebrate
we go to the
border of california
and nevada
and buy lottery tickets
to try to win money
we will
never see in our life
it's me and her
because we are 18
a rite of passage
to start gambling
on the lottery
to take a chance
to have a good laugh
to be disappointed
when it doesn't go our way
to say okay
maybe next time
to have an adventure
to have a story to tell

GIRLS BEING GIRLS

getting ready to take pictures in the backyard
this outfit- no this one!
how about this one?
does my makeup look good?
should i put eyeliner on?
oh this yes!
that outfit is good.
we are so lucky you have this camera!
girls clamoring over one another,
arms legs everywhere.
faces in mirrors being examined, applied to,
laughter, gossip, tears.
intensity like it's NYFW.
we have got to get this right!
this is the vibe i'm going for,
oh pass me that lipstick!
wait should i wear lipstick?
girls being girls.

FREEDOM TO BE

feeling free and light
meeting in the center of the school
9:55 ready to eat out
all of us rushing to our cars
debating where to eat like anything
but ihop and denny's isn't open yet
free in the freedom of accomplishing something
then having the whole day ahead

18 AS TOLD BY REBECCA PART ?

when you're 18 and you're at the in-n-out and your ex boyfriend who you sometimes have sex with is coming out, you say hello. you then proceed to get your drunk friend and bring her back to your house. when you're 18, he snapchats you and asks if you want to smoke and then have sex. you're 18 and you like both of those things, so you say yes. when he gets there, you come out in a sweatshirt and your underwear and get in his car. you take three hits off the wood. your mind starts to slow to a pace you've never seen before. your body feels unsteady and lopsided. when he is done smoking, you guys go to get out of the car. you trip but catch yourself. he asks if you can make it to the door or if you need help. you're 18 and you can do anything. you tell him you can make it. you do make it but you're stumbling. you can't feel your feet and everything is kinda spinning slowly. your depth perception is definitely off. you make it inside but you have to hold onto the walls to guide you through the dark hallway. you're 18 and something is wrong. you're high though. so high nothing is computing. when you guys make it to your room at the back of the hallway you go and get in your bed. you feel terrible and uneasy. your body has now been confined to the bed. you're 18 and you're wondering what the hell is going on. when he starts to move you, you want to say no but you find you can't find your voice. when you're 18 and you're high out of your mind you have an out of body experience. you are watching him over you. you don't really know what is happening. you can't say no out loud. your brain is a low hum. all you hear is no. when it's over you fall asleep. you're 18 and you wake up to an alarm the next morning. it's him saying he has to go. so he does and you feel disgust looking at him. you can't place why. when you wake up later you immediately feel the need to shower. when you're 18 and you shower for 45 minutes on a random saturday in november, you start to feel as if something is wrong.

CAN YOU HEAR ME?

i scream until i can't feel my throat.
                                but it falls on deaf ears.

i try and play the game to achieve what needs to be done
              and feel nothing but dirt when it's done.

i feel naked in the middle of a theatre full of people
             but I still feel like they are staring past me.
like calling a name over and over to find you're being
ignored.

             i   am   not   seen.   I   am   not   heard.
                   i am talking to a brick wall.
the look of indifference plagues me,
haunts my dreams and when i wake up it's there to greet me.

i am constantly
             falling
          between
       anger and sadness

wanting to be understood.
no matter what i do, it never makes it through.

IS YOUR BRAIN ON FIRE TOO?

my brain is   spinning
i've lost my   bearing
my
  brain
    wants
      out
       of
       my
         HEAD
  i think i'm going mad

IT'S MY LIFE

smoking cigarettes   eating so little
late nights   earlier mornings
                oh is my life precious?
it's such a   fickle   thing
                            that i must stay alive
when it's so much easier to die
            oh is my life precious?
i must have   reminders   on what it is to be alive
i need to touch
                  feel
                    to know what's real
everything seems so   shiny   and   unreal
            oh is my life precious?

18 AS TOLD BY REBECCA PART ?

at 18 you finally see the boy who has been trying to get your attention. it comes at a bad time. he is talking to another girl. you don't care though. they aren't boyfriend and girlfriend. you decide he is going to be your boyfriend. you start spending time together and you're flirting. he flirts back. you tell him that if this is going anywhere, he has to stop talking to the other girl. he does. you keep talking and flirting. one day, you ask him when he is gonna ask you to be his girlfriend. when you're 18, you're confident. he asks you right then. you say yes even if you think it's not romantic.

December

18 AS TOLD BY REBECCA PART ?

it's christmas time and you're 18. you have to get a gift for your best friend. you go to the smoke shop looking for a bong. you find the cutest blubber you ever did see. it's red and small and adorable. you buy it. when it's christmas time when you're 18, you exchange gifts, just the two of you. she gets you a ring and you give her the bubbler. She loves it. She says you have to break it in with her and smoke it. you've never taken well to glass but you figure that was just pipes. when you're 18 you break in the bubbler. you get so high, when you close your eyes you feel like you are in the emoji movie when they get lost in the data. only it's your memories. then your brain stops and picks one. you're 18 in your best friend's bed and your brain starts to play the last time you got high. this time, instead of being above it, you are in your body and you feel it. the thrusts, his breath over your ear, him moving you into the positions he wants. you're 18 when you feel sick. it's building in your stomach. you feel the acid moving around. then a thrust happens. you feel it pierce your bowels and you feel the puke travel up your esophagus. you sit up in a rush and puke over the side of the bed onto the hardwood floor. your best friend is startled. you start to cry profusely. you're 18 when you have a nightmare while awake.

PHYSICAL ILLNESS MEETING
METAPHORICAL SILENCE

my throat is raw
                i have been coughing for days
it   almost   makes me laugh
           then i cough
the cycle repeats
i'm   laughing because
              i can barely speak
my throat is so   raw
how the things we take for   granted
sometimes i have the feeling i'm not speaking loud enough for
people to hear me
now i can barely speak at all
            i really am whispering
when i   laugh   i   cough
now i have no choice but to not speak
no one can hear me now

WINTER CLEANING

uncompromising. everything must go. the glass smash it.
take the bat and clear the shelves. the clothes burn them.
leave nothing out. the books you can donate those. the bed
the sheets cut them up then burn them. destroy everything in
the room. clean the walls with acid. pick up the bat again and
smash the furniture. everything must be destroyed. everything.
must. be. destroyed.

THIS IS THE DESCENT

(into madness
and rage
and envy
and sadness
and bitterness
and always a dull ache)

DO HAVE A CHAPSTICK I COULD BORROW?

my lips are chapped
i lick them when i'm anxious or sad
they stay chapped
because i can't leave my room
where i don't have any chapstick
i am in a squared confinement that is my room
due to my own willingness to not leave and brave the world
all i need is water i have no appetite
some chapstick would be stellar
i just would need to move
and my body is 1000s of pounds
instead i lick and bite and taste blood
that's what i eat
it taste like metallic but it's an almost satisfying taste

DIFFERENT PERSPECTIVE

she hasn't been the same since ya know? something changed. she moves on edge like everything is out to get her. i don't know how to get through to her. no one can touch her. i asked her what that was about. she just got fire in her eyes but also looked like she was about to cry. i don't know what to do with that. she's colder now, words wielded to cut. she went and got a dragon tattoo on her ribs. then a tattoo on her sternum. it's like she's looking for pain. i don't know man, i can't get through to her. i think i'm gonna quit it.

HOME REMEDIES

going to puke my intestines into a bowl
fill it with water and boil it. peel my skin inch by inch and
lay it out in the sun. take my brain out and fan the flames
that are on it. lay my bones in the grass next to a tree. once a
week every week for one year. this will cure the twisting, the
touches, the memories, and lastly the aches.

RE: #57

in response to #57 in bang! by rollins.

a girl has got a gun. she stares at her hand. she stares at the gun. deliberating about what to do and who to shoot. herself? no, her rapist. yes, yes, yes. him of course. load it up, take off the safety. take aim. got a round and all of the bullets have his name. a girl has got a gun. she stares at her hand. she stares at the gun. mind made up. she stares at him.

THE GIRL YOU HAD BEFORE IS GONE

don't you see what you did? you killed her. she now ceases
to exist. here and there now everywhere. she is gone. the last
thread, the innocence, now taken. she is dead and will be born
new again. something different. will look the same but will be
different. you killed her. the girl you knew is gone. everyone
will wonder where she went and why she's acting different.
all thanks to you. it will take some time but she won't know
either. she will spend years deciphering who she is with who
she was. all because you killed her. how cruel of you to kill
a girl for selfish pleasure. how demented and twisted of you
to treat her the same as before. as if you weren't the cause of
panic inducing nightmares of coming back from the dead. how
truly sickening you are indeed.

I HOPE YOU ROT

you are nosebleeds
and fleas
and droughts in the desert
you are rotten fish in the trash
you are the rash that won't fade
you are the sand stuck in crevices the sun don't shine in
you are that irritating fly buzzing around you
you are the paper cut on the pointer finger
you are the test you know you're going to fail
you are the sun waking you up when you're suppose to sleep in
you are the child that screams and will never quit
you are the gum stuck on the bottom of the shoe
you are that song that plays over and over on the radio

THE OTHER

i don't feel real
my body is distorted
my thoughts are deeply scattered
deeply miserable and bleeding into one another

when i look in the mirror i do not see myself
rather an imposter
my hair isn't laying as it should
my eyes look downward even when i'm looking
straight ahead

i am not here nor there
i am nowhere
far away from my person
i do not even like where i am
it is dark and secluded

i feel anxious and unsure of what's happening
i can't make sense of anything
it is all dark and dreary

purgatory.

45 MINUTES IN THE SHOWER OKAY

water rushing down on to you.
        body red,   hot.
you've scrubbed   scrubbed   scrubbed.

feeling the need   to   claw   your skin off.
yes,   let's claw it off.
dragging nails up your legs.   you feel the skin under your
finger nails.   relief.

not enough. the blood is prickling   on your legs.   arms.
let's do the arms.
peel   peel   peel. blood oozing   slowly.
skin under your   fingernails.

stomach next.   you'll have marks all
                                                    over.
you   will be   clean keep going.
hands pruning. water is turning cold.
you're   running   out of   time.

you will have to go   back   later.

I'M STAYING STILL

i cannot feel my body
it is as if it is not my own
i feel like crying but no tears come out
i am unable to move
my mouth will not form words
i feel far and removed from the world
staring at it through an impenetrable glass window
i feel simply lifeless

18 AS TOLD BY REBECCA PART ?

when you're 18, you get cast as a lead in the school play. you're ecstatic. you feel on top of the world. there is nothing you can't do. talent is what you're dealing with. your first time auditioning and you make a lead. your vow to be there in theatre is paying off and since you can't direct you are acting. you feel a bit typecast but you're not too worried about it. you go to the read through and you read your lines. when you're 18, you just feel so happy to be a part of something. you forget everything else that is going on and feel elevated like you're at the entrance of a cage about to fly free. when you're 18, it's a dangerous feeling, but you try to grasp it.

TRAPPING

i! am! moving slow! thinking fast!
i. am. very sad. feeling numb.
i. think. i need to scream! nothing is coming out.

my! mouth! is wide open! i'm not making a sound!
i. am. falling to my knees. begging for release.
i. am. trapped inside my body! warped in thoughts.

WEIGHTLESS AND HEAVY BUT CAN YOU HEAR ME

i am weightless in thought
heavy in body
drifting but my feet touch the ground every so often
i am big and bright and everything lovely
then i am dull and dim waiting to ignite
i cannot fathom that my life must go on
that there is more
what am i searching for
what is there i haven't seen

i am weightless in thought
heavy in body
going about my day
trying to find meaning
trying to hold onto passion
fighting to be able to love
fighting myself at every turn
just to be balanced in mind
balanced in body

LITTLE GREEN COLOR ME IN ENVY

there are three sprite cans lined
                                        up
                                          diagonally
on my side table

i have shelves
            of
        books
i have decided to keep
some of them read   some of them not

   my tv hangs up on the wall centered
            above my record player
i have a suitcase and a closet   the doors to it remain
closed

there are clothes on the
                        floor

all my hair products are   behind   my mirror

my bed is a mess of blankets   pillows i don't use
books i'm currently   reading   some journals

i live in my room so fully it is a nest of me
me and my sweet little green walled room

THIS IS TIME PASSING SLOWLY, QUICKLY, PASSING

my days are blurring together
one by one
week by week
it is all one stretch of time
day bleeds to night
and night into morning
all one never ending

SAD/MAD SAME THING NO?

i feel it in my head
my tears keep creeping in
i am a ticking time bomb
i am going to explode
it's always late at night
when i feel myself slipping away
i can't escape
i am a prisoner to my own mind
i cannot get out even when i try
it bangs on me
sends punch after punch
i am incredibly sad
i am incredibly mad
i cannot get out of my head
a part of me dies every time
what do i do when there is nothing left?

SHE DOESN'T EVEN HAVE A SUICIDE NOTE

there's a gun, rope, and bricks. she doesn't care how she goes. just that she's got to go. the gun has the potential to leave too much room for nerves. a messy clean up too. blowing your brains out like that. maybe she's too pretty for it. the rope. what an idea. she just doesn't know how she can rig it. rather mathematical for an english lit girl. she will think on it. the bricks. tied to her ankles then into the pool she goes. her legs are strong though. she might be able to kick them off. the more she thinks about it, the more it seems to not pan out. she'll have to go back to the drawing board. more ways to go about going away. so maybe she does care how she goes. either way she still has to go.

January

YOU HONESTLY MAKE ME PUKE

acidic in my stomach
churning round and round
bile rising
sick coming up
through the esophagus
out my mouth
every time i even think of you.

THIS COMPANY SUCKS

i am hollowed out in pain
it colors me purple
it bleeds from me
and when i walk people avoid me
they can't see it
but it radiates
they stay away
i am bitter and miserable
all i want is to be pulled near
yet it keeps me far away
how we have fallen
to not help the weak and miserable
and instead stay far away
invisible barrier
you don't know why
disease you don't want to catch
bitterness and misery
they are all i have for company

DEATH IS TALKING TO ME

fear has no place here
give in
give in
let go and enjoy the ride
there is only one destination
everyone gets there eventually
you're just going to get there soon
i promise it will be worth it
you'll even have a say
isn't that so fun
you get to choose it
ultimately i can veto it
but i know you'll come up with the best idea
give in
give in
let go and enjoy the ride

18 AS TOLD BY REBECCA PART ?

when you're 18 and you're driving you and your boyfriend to school, a car will pull out in front of you. you'll swerve. your boyfriend will pull the oh shit handle. you already aren't speaking, but you won't speak after it happens. almost like it didn't happen. when you're 18, you'll pull into your parking spot at school and put the car in park. then you'll look over at your boyfriend. we almost got in a car accident, you'll say. he'll shake his head like he's ridding himself of the thought, and then agree and say it was crazy. when you're 18, you'll realize how easy it is to die and how hard it is to fight the instinct to stay alive.

I AM FIGHTING A WAR IN ME

but i am stationary
i am not getting anywhere
i am suffering in my head
dreading my self
for not being stronger than my mind

THE FIRST TIME IN THE ABYSS WAS VERY UNPLEASANT TO BE HONEST

i thought that i was picky
then you picked me and i let you
fell into your arms with my arms crossed
faced forward
you caught me
held me just for moment
till you let go and sent me flying
into an abyss
falling falling falling
never ending
thoughts never ceasing
wondering how i misjudged
how i got into the black of night
no sun no light
me alone
full of regret

CASSY!!!!!

these people make me feel not real.
i can't tell if it's them or me.
you make me feel real though.
i always feel like a real person after talking to you.
they never understand anything I say.
they don't laugh at my jokes,
they don't get that i'm sad in my bones.
save me cassy please!
i'll beg on my hands and knees.
what will it take to get you here?
i know i said i'd never ask
it's just that i'll rip my hair out
if you don't.
it's harder than i thought.
being so far from you.
i know we will talk soon,
it's just that i need you now.
at least tell me i'm real!

PYROMANIACS DEATH

what if i were to ask you to light me on   fire
would   you   do   it?

if i told you   let   me   burn   this is how i want to go
would   you   let   me?

what if
        i told you
                    if   you   don't   i
                                    will?
            this is the escape

  this   is   my   last   wish

i want to burn out.

  i want to be bright one   last
                                    time.

DO YOU HAVE A PLACE FOR ME TO STAY?

i do not feel anything at all
i feel dull and useless
taking up space
unable to find the thing that will give meaning
i am a body in a home
looking for somewhere to go
looking for something to do

I'D LIKE TO SPEAK WITH A DOCTOR

i think i need a doctor. one to examine my brain. you see, it is going a bit haywire. i'm feeling out of control. my thoughts are fast passing. nothing is going on. it feels lit on fire. also, i'm not sleeping enough. very little indeed. i think that if i went to a doctor i'd tell him i couldn't even believe i was there. nothing feels real. i feel out of my body you see. yes like i'm not really here at all. i keep seeing myself walking like i'm an angel watching over someone. i fear i don't like what i see either. poor run down girl. skinny, pale, and very tired. everyone is passing her by. you'd think they'd know a cry for help when they saw one. i'd tell the doctor i'm unwell, is it usual to hear death in your ear? maybe i'll write a letter to a doctor. yes, i'll start with dear doctor, why do i keep thinking of guns and ropes and bricks? why do i argue with everyone to feel alive? i don't know when but i think i ate electricity. i feel like a million watts are coursing through me at all times. could you help me doctor? could you tell me what's happening to me? i fear something is very wrong with me doctor. please get back to me at your earliest convenience. sincerely, rebecca

I'M SORRY, I'M SORRY, I'M REALLY TRULY SORRY

cruel intentions
were never apart of me

but-
the more I   stewed
                brewed
                    bled

It became part of my
            language
                thoughts
                    body

now they are subconscious
make them hurt just to see
make them feel you
in the worst way

YOU'RE WORKING OVERTIME, RELAX.

i'd like to take my brain out of my head
cut open my head

take out my brain
put it in water

bathe it lovingly
massage it gently

tell it
"i know you work so hard"

let it know
that i know it does so much

my brain needs a break
i want to bathe it

so please let me try
oh please let me try

PLEASE TELL ME YOU FEEL LIKE I DO

i look inside me and see nothing
when i peel my skin
there is nothing there
when i yank my head open
it is empty
when i walk i see people with smiles
and i envy how they move through their lives
with a smile on their face
for a second i wonder if they are just like me

MY INSIDES ARE TOUCHING MY OUTSIDES ON THE WRONG SIDE

my inside are coiling up
taking dives into themselves
there is swooping and tumbling going on
i can feel every little move
it's making me sick
it's coming out both ends
i feel violently ill
there's no thrill

A GIRL ISN'T A GUN, BUT SHE'S GOT A GUN

so you've got the gun. you ask yourself what you're even doing with it. you don't know. you just found it. you didn't even go looking for it. it's like it just came to you. were you meant to have this gun? so you've got the gun. you think it's meant for you. you don't know what you're going to do with it. *save me for later*, it whispers. so you save it for later. for just in case. for when you get the nerve. for when the day comes. for when it's time.

THIS IS YOUR CAPTAIN SPEAKING

we are currently experiencing unforeseen turbulence. the
seatbelt sign has been turned on, please buckle up. you may
want to hold onto the arm handles or the hand of a loved one,
or anyone. it is about to get bumpy. i want you all to know this
is my first time in turbulence as bad as this so please bear with
me at this time. i will be doing my very best to get us through
it safely.

18 AS TOLD BY REBECCA PART ?

you're 18, and you are getting down to the wire about rehearsing without scripts. this is a problem for you because you can't seem to remember your lines no matter how much you and your partner read them together. with every day that passes, you feel more jittery. death is knocking on your door telling you to play. telling you there's other things more important. you're trying so hard to retain what you read. what you say aloud. it's just not happening. you and your scene partner are on your bed going over the lines and you feel like you're getting them, but it doesn't matter then. what matters is if you remember them on stage. when you're 18, you're forgetting a lot of things. you can't place anything, let alone your lines for the school play. you're having trouble recalling anything at all. you're getting agitated more than you're not. your boyfriend is being weird. you're being weird. everything is coming down around you. when you're 18 you can't remember your fucking lines.

NO CAFFEINE JUST ELECTRICITY

every   smile   looks
    d e r a n g e d
and   i   feel   it   by   the
                                                    day

my   eyes
      b l o w n
look too
      w   i   d   e
yet   tired   at   the   same   time
i've got purple
underneath

my   lips   chapped
from
chewing
licking
making them bleed

my   hands   permanently   shake
electricity   buzzing   through veins
a   f   u   r   r   y   brain
overloading
not computing

i   can't   retain   new   information
and i'm forgetful on a   good   day
completely s   h   o   c   k   e   d   on a bad one
yes   i'm   losing   it   completely   i think

NO WAY, YOU'RE JUST HAPPY

i've never been a jealous person
when i see people happy however
i fill to the brim with indignation
i do not understand it
it must be false
it cannot be true
if it were true
why don't i have it?

MECHANICAL ENGINEERING

i've never been interested-

but when i look in the mirror

tilt my head side to side

up and down

then poke my eye

stand up and pose

raise my arm above my head

walk back and forth

put my hands on my hips

try to smile

it all seems very robotic

I THINK I'M DRIVING ME INSANE

running
running fast
through a maze
no ending in sight
keep running into dead ends
shallow breaths pumping through
hands on knees
trapped in a maze
never ending
more like a labyrinth
trap doors
dead ends that lead to doors
step through
different world new problems
still a labyrinth
still running
puffing shallow breaths
fall through the floor
twisted ankle
get up test it out
pain feels good
running running
through the labyrinth
that is the mind

MY TEETH KEEP FALLING OUT

sometimes in my dreams
my teeth fall   out
        and i wake up in a   panic
when i look it up it says
that it symbolizes   anxiety
                        insecurity
                            or   loss
when i wake
i check to see i have
                    all my teeth
then i remind myself to   brush   my   teeth
make an appointment   with   the   dentist
                maybe never sleep again

EVERYONE AND THING IS LAUGHING
AT ME

i'm trying
       to get
my head
     on straight
it's proving
       difficult it
keeps squirming
      around and
twisting this
     way and
that way
      facing my
back saying
      now i've
really got
      eyes in
the back
      and a
nose and
      a mouth
hah take
      that!

THE MADNESS IS OVERTAKING ME

choking on my sadness
lying in my madness
eyes wide open
tears falling without my knowing
life playing on repeat through my mind
what a life that has given in to madness

ALWAYS A DOLL, NEVER A REAL LIFE GIRL

hollow remains
carved out
wooden doll
not russian
just one
one hollow
doll looking
in the
mirror wondering
how she
got made
thinking of
what it
had to
take to
hollow her
out and
the make
up on
her face
painted on
to look
like a
smile
it's all
an illusion

February

YOU'RE UNFORGETTABLE BUT I'LL SPEND THE REST OF MY LIFE TRYING TO FORGET YOU

when i see even a glimpse of you i feel full of rage and disgust. it's so deep within me my insides curl and hurl. it's a visceral reaction. the way they shrivel and shrink. my brain screams kill kill kill. run run run. give him a taste of the end of your fist. you see, i go to war every time i even think of you. if it was your goal to never be forgotten, i think you succeeded. you've succeeded and i've suffered the consequences of your actions. not everyone is willing or capable of committing an unforgivable act to be remembered.

18 AS TOLD BY REBECCA PART ?

when you're 18 and you don't remember anything at all, it makes the day-to-day harder. your grades are slipping, your friends are getting irritated. you're arguing to hell and back. when you're 18, you think you're losing your mind. you don't know what to do. you wonder if it will come back. death whispers in your ear. you try to bat it away, but it is very persistent. you feel like running 90 miles. you feel like climbing a mountain no one ever has. you're jittery and twitchy. when you're 18, all you see when you look in the mirror is a pale face and jet black eyes pupils blown wide. you twist your head and tilt it. touch your face and wish for it to be over. this never ending rage and misery. when you're 18 looking in the mirror with a distaste for your own face, you fear it will never end.

THIS TIME A GIRL IS NOT A GUN, BUT SHE'S GOT ONE AND THIS TIME SHE'S THINKING OF YOU

i've got a gun. i've got suicidal ideation. more importantly, i've got a list. your name is in bold and underlined. i've got a gun. nothing is too far. i have a problem and i have a solution. it is all very logical. i've got a gun. i've got a list. i've been a victim of an unforgivable act. they whisper that murder, yes murder, can be justified. you on the other hand, they say you deserve what's coming to you. i've got a gun. i've got a thirst to even the playing field. most importantly, i'd just feel better with you dead.

I KEEP BREAKING THINGS AND I DON'T FEEL ANY BETTER

grab the glass.
smash the glass.
find another.
do it again,
and again,
and again.
let out the never ending rage.
the rage that consumes you so whole.
the rage that won't leave you alone.
the rage that makes you want to cause destruction.

grab the plate.
smash the plate.
find another.
do it again,
and again,
and again.
let out the never ending rage.
the rage that intensifies.
the rage that makes you scream into the night.
the rage that whistles and sings.

grab the bowl.
smash the bowl.
find another.
do it again,
and again,
and again.
let out the never ending rage.

the rage that has buried you.
the rage that keeps you up day and night.
the rage that is going to kill you.

18 AS TOLD BY REBECCA PART ?

when you're 18, there is so much going on. you're stopping, though. you don't know what's happening but you can feel yourself emptying. more accurately, like you have been turned to a different setting. you feel angry and rageful. you want to argue every little thing, so you do. you feel jumpy in your skin. it's taking everything in you to contain it. you have thoughts that are faster than a cheetah attacking. when you're 18, you start thinking of death a lot. you think something of it but you don't at the same time. when you're 18, you develop a lack of apathy towards your own life. live or die, you don't care. when you're in your room, you hate everything and wish for rest. you feel violent and volatile. almost like anything might make you explode. you have a taste for things that are fast. dangerous. your mind is going a mile a minute. you can't retain any information. when you're 18, at first you think it's teenage angst. then you think, this is what i've been telling them for years. the depression, the anxiety. this is what it's all been leading to. when you're 18, you think it to be your last. you'll leave it up to chance for a while, though.

I CAN'T GET RID OF THE BITTERNESS

there's a bitter taste in my mouth
like i've just eaten something tart
it stays with me day and night
as i move through life
these days pass but they bleed
i always have this taste
it's strong when people look at me and say nothing
when they hug me but let go too quickly
when they tell me my life is so nice
that they like my house, i'm so lucky
tart bitter acidic
hanging out in my mouth, i have to spit it out
sometimes it's bearable
sometimes i have to brush and brush
just to taste something else crawl through my body
watching, seeing, everyone around me
the love and hugs
the relationships and kisses
the laughs and stolen glances
i sit miserable talking to death
as my only companion
envious that others have full life
while i near the end of mine

SORRY FOR TAKING YOU FOR GRANTED

when i can't sleep   i go to the floor

i don't know what good it does me
it makes me miss my bed

so   i   lay   on   the   floor
so that i take my bed for   granted

when i've had enough of the
                    hard   itchy   carpet
i go back to my bed and i fall asleep

THE INTERTWINING OF ME

in my sadness
i become intertwined with pain
it becomes vivid and illustrated
in deep black and white with heavy grays
there is no color in my sadness
the world has lost its shine
i am living in a silent film
i cannot even hear my own wails of pain
how unfortunate for i
who loves color
who loves when time moves quickly
to be so paralyzed by a sorrow so bone deep

TIME IS CONSTANT AND ALWAYS THERE

my days are blurring together
one by one
week by week
it is all one stretch of time
day bleeds to night
and night into morning
all one, never ending

TWO THINGS AT ONCE

my head is pounding
like hammers drumming on my skull

i have this sensation of falling
every time i lift one foot in front of the other

i'm on the precipice of something
i can feel it

i feel heavy
yet light

free
yet shackled

my vision is going in and out
everything is dancing before me

jumping here and there
not staying still

DO YOU THINK I'M PRETTY?

i am clawing at my face
my nails are scraping from the top of my forehead
down to the bottom of my chin
i can feel the dead skin beneath my nails
it is not enough i need my skin to come off
all of it
i go faster, then clawing quickly
without abandon

my face is red as the sun
with claw marks on it
as i stare in the mirror
i feel beautiful
my outside matches my inside
there's little pools of blood
from where i scratched so deep

it is both perfect and not yet enough
my face is tender to the touch
raw
it will have to do for now

18 AS TOLD BY REBECCA PART ?

when you're 18 and life has thrown you a tsunami you can't swim in, you don't think anything of it when your friend says she's been feeling ill. nauseous, to be exact. when you're 18 and you don't smoke weed anymore but your friend does it everyday, you tell them that's why you feel ill. you're smoking too much. even though it's recommended to help with nausea. your friend gives you an exasperated look. when you're 18, there are a lot of secrets that are kept in a group of girls. just because you haven't graduated high school yet. you don't know it because you're the oldest you've ever been, but you are not mature in the slightest. when you're 18 and you made a bet with your friend that you could not have sex with your boyfriend for three months, you aren't really thinking of other people having sex. it's your world, darling. when you're 18 and your friend who has claimed nausea opens your car door in the morning to puke her guts outside of it, you think it's gross and uncalled for. what the hell is wrong with you. it happens again outside the vape store. you don't smoke weed, but you do smoke nicotine. some call it hypocrisy. you are 18 though. you have had sex. you have heard stories. even though your own life is taking you on a high speed ride through all of america, you pause. the clogs in your brain start turning, albeit slowly. then you feel stupid. your stomach drops. you feel like the floor is moving. *have you taken a pregnancy test?* you ask. it feels surreal. teen pregnancy. a baby. so your friend takes the test and it's positive. when you're 18, there are a lot of secrets. so it takes a while to figure out who the dad is. you bring up options. when you're 18, you're self centered. you start to think if this happened to you. a thing growing in you. taking your nutrients. kicking you in the stomach. making you puke every morning. your stomach enlarging til you waddle. then you think you're gonna be sick. when you're 18, it seems that life is just getting too real.

ASLEEP OR AWAKE LIFE IS A NIGHTMARE

there's dark circles under my eyes that are purple and blue like i've been bruised

they stand out on my pale face that has lost its color fully

i am in a right state staying awake just to not have nightmares

there's caffeine running through my veins just to keep me awake

i'm full of fear, from the ends of my hair down to the ends of my toenails, it consumes me

jumpy from the caffeine, paranoid from lack of sleep

walking through life petrified there is no peace awake or asleep

18 AS TOLD BY REBECCA PART ?

when you're 18 and filled with rage, spending everyday with other high schoolers, you have a short fuse. you're seeing red more than you're not. you're screaming as loud as you can, yet everyone keeps passing you by. something is very wrong. when you're 18 and you feel the call for death, you wish someone would pull you back. you're arguing over stupid things. you're drinking excessively. you're not sleeping. you can't calm your mind no matter what. it is constantly coming up with something new. when you're 18, you think about punching anything and everything. you think to yourself, you should get in a fight. you think you could win it. in your head, death is the only win. you try to keep yourself in check. when you're 18, you want to smash everything in sight. blow money you don't have. kiss everyone and watch them fall dead. you want to carve yourself out. you feel like a shadow of yourself. when you're 18, you don't know where you've gone.

TWO WRONGS TO EQUAL SELF PRESERVATION

you have turned me into a guiltless creature. my words sting and burn. yet i smile. it feels good. you have made me cruel towards others because i know nothing else. i bask in the shock, in the hurt of the emotions that filter through their faces, trying to decide how they feel. it makes me feel light. it is sinister. sometimes i feel like clawing it out of me, but if i did you would hurt me. i cannot be hurt anymore.

DON'T LET ME BE ALONE IN THIS MISERY

i am not clawing
it is clawing
from my insides
crawling up me
through my throat
out my mouth
i spew green acid
burning those around me
i am miserable
be miserable too

HOW DID YOU END UP IN MY BED?

feeling trapped inside my skin
like i need to peel it off to get out
all i can hear is *i don't want to*
it plays on repeat in my head
it starts as a whisper then louder and louder

i squirm in my bed knowing it's been occupied by another
being
it makes me want to wash my body ten times over
burn the sheets, the pillows
get rid of every reminder

feeling trapped and restless
pressure after confession
like a daisy in the wind you said the wrong thing but now i
feel bad
i can't stand my ground
you didn't even make a good point

now all i have is regret
the feeling to flee from my own life
it's suffocating me
i'm clawing at my skin
i can't get clean

LET ME DRIVE THE HIGH SPEED TRAIN

i'm going to jump out of my skin
fuck it
i'm going to find the tallest building and climb
i have this need
this need
this need
i don't know what to do with it
i'll swim all the oceans
i'll bike around the world
i need
something
anything
light me on fire
i'll stop drop and roll
something has to be done
i'm filling to the brim with energy
i'm stuck staring at a wall
get me out
free me
i can't be doomed to this life
i need
tell me something pretty
so i don't lose my mind
i need something gritty
something that fits just right
something raw
that i can sink my teeth in to
i need to feel it in my bones
that swoop in my stomach
i need

18 AS TOLD BY REBECCA PART ?

when you're 18, you are filled with such rage you don't know what to do with yourself. you feel like you are the almighty and everyone should be bowing to you. you feel like you can do anything at all. you feel like you could look death in the eye and it would shudder. you think you're invincible. you are just so angry. when you're 18, you look around your room. you need to do something, anything at all. you look at your paintings on canvas, and you think bingo. when you're 18, everyone else is out of the house. you go up to your canvas and you stare at it. then you put your fist through it. hard. 27 times. when you're 18 and you've finished doing that, your hand is swollen and bruising purple. you smile and think, oh good. you're 18 when you realize what they mean when they ask if you want to hurt yourself.

I'LL PLAY A DANGEROUS GAME, I'VE GOT NOTHING TO LOSE

hit me again
i can't feel it
from what i can tell it feels great
don't you know i'm already in pain
everything feels the same
hit me again

put a knife to my throat
i'll tell you to cut
i've been escaping death
you won't cut
i'll be having a thrill
put a knife to my throat

i think i'll put my hand on the stove
they tell you not to
natural curiosity of a child
i feel like i know everything and nothing at all
i'll just leave it there till i smell it burning
people will ask about it and i'll be blaśe
maybe i'll tell wild stories
i think i'll put my hand on the stove

walk in to the street
i didn't look both ways
If someone hits me i'll die or end up at college
the cars are coming but so i am
always the right away unless
unless no not unless
no one wants to be a murderer
walk in to the street

living life like everyday i'll die
pain and pleasure intertwine
this is where i find my divine

YOU SEE, I HAD A RUN IN WITH A MIRROR

a police officer came to the door. he knocked. i looked through the peephole. i slowly opened the door. *how can i help you officer?* he told me they had gotten noise complaints. *couldn't have been me officer, i'm all alone.* he told me that i needed to keep it down. he didn't want to come back. anything officer, have a good night. he walked down the drive and i closed the door. as i made my way to the stairs, i grabbed my hammer. i made it to the attic and close the door. i locked eyes across the room. me and the mirror. i rose my arm with the hammer and took my aim. i released it. i heard blaring shatters. then i screamed and hoped my ears would bleed. i wandered into the middle of the room and twirled in a circle. i screamed every time i caught a glimpse, and prayed for it all to be over.

YES, YOU ARE IN FACT GOING CRAZY

control
thoughts and thoughts
40 per second, 45 per second
60 per second, 70 per second
too many to count per second
ever growing, never slowing
only constant is that i'm losing my mind

IT'S DEPRESSION, I'M NOT LAZY

i lay in bed staring at the ceiling
no thoughts
just space

feeling empty
i've been burned, all that remains is ash
in and out of paralyzing thoughts
days pass and i haven't moved

no peace
too many thoughts
i lay in bed staring at the ceiling

COIN TOSS

I need more time.
My head is bursting
                 flaming
                       trickling.
I'm on the brink of death
                    insanity
I   am   Immortal
I am the great of all greats
I can do whatever I please
I cannot fail.
I need more time.
I need more time.
Why is time falling away from me?
Why are the days gray?
Why am I lonely?
Where did the colors go?
Is it me?
I am slowly   fading
                  withering
                    melting
I need more time.
I need more time.
I'm swimming
         I'm drowning.
                I'm underwater.
I can't breathe.
I can't breathe.
I can't breathe.
I can't die
I have too much too much too much

Too much what?
What am I thinking?
Why can't I remember?
I need more time.
I need more time.
Where am I?
Why am I so lost?
How did I get here?
I hate my life.
I don't deserve to be here.
Everyone is much happier than me.
They couldn't live without me if they tried.
I am the greatest great.
Everyone bows to me.
I am meant to be the best.
I need more time.
There are not enough hours in the day.
The sun sets and rises
                              I have not slept.
The moon appears and disappears
                                   I have not slept.
My head is so full,
                but my soul,
                      my soul has gone
                              somewhere else.
I am a shell of existence.
I am better off dead.
Where did everyone go?
You need no one, they need you.
 I am the greatest great.
I need more time.
I can't leave yet.

I need more time.
 I can't leave my bed.
The days are too long.
The wall has not changed.
I feel like I haven't blinked.
Nothing matters anymore.
I need more time
To overcome,
            To achieve,
                    to be the best.
What is happening to me?
Where am I?
How did I end up here?
Everything is gray
                getting darker by the day.
My soul is dying,
            my head is flaming.
I need more time.
I need more time.
I need more time.
I need more time.
I need.
I need.
I.

VITRIOL POURING OUT

i cannot contain it
my mouth moves
before i can stop it
i say the most heinous thing
from deep within
i hit you in your chest
you stare at me speechless
i feel pleased and delighted
that i could come up with something so mean

A GIRL IS NOT THE GUN, A GIRL IS THE BULLET

the bullet in the gun
that's what i am

shoot me out, i'm a speeding bullet
i'll hit you in the heart and knock you dead

i'll come out clean the other side
blood on me
lost in the debris

GOODBYE GOODBYE

the abyss is calling my name
whispering in my ear
it's seducing me
i have no control of my feet
it sounds so sweet
pretty, even neat
telling me i can burn it all down
ashes all around
they won't call me insane
they are just like me
they are calling my name
cheering me on, it sounds like
and i'm going to go
i will see you from the other side
tears in your eyes

March

I THINK YOU'RE A SCUMBAG

i wish you'd be more considerate
that was never your thing
but i still wish it
i wished it most
when you took me in your hands
and moved me to your will
to satisfy your needs
how my body became just a body
i think this because my mind was not working
you would have taken me anyway
awake, asleep, intoxicated, sober
it didn't matter, you had a single mind
and for this i will hate you forever
your lack of consideration makes me sick

ENVY IN THE MORNING

when i wake, the sun has not risen. much like i have not risen.
i lay there and contemplate. thinking of taking on the days
puts a smile on my face. thinking of how everyone will laugh,
but I'll never know what's funny. how everyone is moving
through life but i am still in rushing water. i do not understand
how everyone is moving through it. i feel it in the pit of my
stomach, growing green, coloring me. how easy for everyone
else to live when they don't have death in their ear.

DON'T WAKE ME UP

i can't wake up
i'm not even dreaming
but i lull back to sleep
in the confines of my bed
where i was just finding a special kind of sleep
a blank sleep no thoughts running through my brain
i was at perfect rest
then my alarm blared and ruined it
i shut it off with a groan
and resume position
lulling like sleeping meds are in me
this is the closest i've been to death
when i sleep a sleep void of dreams
void of nightmares
and it is so peaceful
i never want to wake from this slumber
don't make it face the day
i won't make it
i'll just be trying to get back

18 AS TOLD BY REBECCA PART ?

when you're 18, your boyfriend hardly breaks up with you properly. when you're 18, you're at a party and he ignores you.you hear through other people that you aren't together. obviously, the only solution is to get wasted. when you're 18, you're in the bathroom at a party. there are two other girls in there with you and you're furious. you think you could put a hole in the wall. when you're 18, you text your boyfriend and tell him if he wants to break up with you he better do it to your face. you go over to his house and he comes outside and sits you on the porch. you confront him. your emotions are running wild. you're desperate, begging, and yelling. he sits there, stoic. when you leave, you cry. it's quickly replaced by anger, which is the only emotion you've been feeling lately. when you're 18 and you get out of your car the next morning, you see your ex boyfriend get out of the car with the girl he told you not to worry about. hot, pure, blue rage filters through your body. when you're 18, you don't know what to do with this anger. you go to class and you're shaking at your desk. the girl is sitting directly across from you. you're looking at her and you feel like you could kill her. when you're 18, you dissociate and you don't see the real world. you see yourself dragging the girl from her desk and punching her bloody on the ground. your hands around her throat, slamming her down. when you're 18 and you come to, you demand for your teacher to let you go to your counselor. when you're 18, you realize what they mean when they ask if you want to hurt others.

MY BRAIN IS ACCESSING THAT OTHER PERCENT THAT'S NEVER USED

rushing rushing
never slowing
i am the high speed train
a million thoughts
zipping around
vying for my attention
it's making me mad with ambition
die   live create
read. write. paint
gamble, you'll win
you're the luckiest girl in the world
go to church
pick up a language
when was the last time you rode a bike?
take up dancing
spend money
kiss everyone
kill someone, you'll get away with it
you'll get away with everything
you are the greatest great

THE REAL TRUTH ABOUT INNOCENCE

they make it seem like you lose your innocence the moment you have sex.

i know this not to be true.

i know that it happens when your voice is trapped and your body is used.

taken into the hands of careless users.

forcefully engaged in acts your mind screams against.

abused by those who know you.

when you are used as a rag doll to meet the wants of others.

yes, i know this now.

18 AS TOLD BY REBECCA PART ?

when you're 18, your friends start a band in december and they practice at your house. you don't play an instrument, you just write the songs. which is equally as important, you'd say. one day it's just you and one member of the band. you guys always work best together. you tell him that you've got to sing. so he brings out his guitar, and you start singing. when you're 18, you always have him play something that you sing to that's how you get your lyrics. you're singing words, and they feel good and true. you sing your heart out and it felt raw. you wish someone would ask if you're okay, but they don't. just that you're talented lyrically. when you're 18, you don't realize you've just sang your suicide note.

I'VE JOINED THE CIRCUS BUT I'M NOT HAVING A GOOD TIME

i am walking on a tightrope
a wire
i can see the other side
in the middle it's getting iffy
it only makes sense to go forward
i'm wobbling
becoming unsteady
i can't turn back
i am so high up
anxiety begins to clench me in my spot

one

foot

in front

of

the

other

just
like
that
keep
going
you'll
make
it
soon

I DON'T REALLY THINK YOU'RE SEEING ME

what do you see when you look at me
surely not a girl that has it all together
surely not a girl with perfect stitched up seams
you see, i'm bursting at them
everything is coming out of me
through my eyes
through my mouth
through my nose
through my fists when they hit

what do you see when you look at me
surely not a girl who hasn't cried recently
surely not a girl who is happy as can be
you see my eyes won't stop leaking
water flows out every night and every morning
salty, never sweet
wet and hot streaking my face
the truth of the matter is, i'm very sad and very mad

what do you see when you look at me
surely not a girl who has perfect grades
surely not a girl who has great attendance
you see i can't concentrate
i don't want to be here or anywhere at all
i want to be gone
maybe drowning
maybe thrown into an abyss

what do you see when you look at me
i can't imagine i don't look a wreck

i'm not hiding, maybe you're not looking
look closer tell me tell me what you see

DREAMLAND DOESN'T WITH THE WAKING

when i sleep
      i dream
        of far away places
                      parallel lives
when i wake up
          i'm filled with lead
               i'm still in a body
                         that is heavy
i'm still in a body
        with a mind that is breaking
                         day
                           by
                            day
   envying the lives of those i dream about

THIS IS THE CRASH LANDING

ladies and gentlemen, captain doom has informed me that we need to prepare the cabin for an emergency landing. your crew is unprepared for this landing so listen very carefully. we are going to crash, but think of it as a landing. we have 1 day to prepare the cabin for landing, so your undivided attention is very important at this time.

18 AS TOLD BY REBECCA PART ?

when you're 18, you go to school. you feel jumpy and out of sorts. you don't trust yourself, yet you have an awfully high opinion of yourself. today, though. if you leave this school, your red car is hitting that wall. you go to first period, hyped on pure nerves and adrenaline. it's coursing through you like tidal waves. you tell your teacher that you need to see your counselor. he asks if it can wait and you tell him absolutely not. you are begging for someone to save you. you make it to your counselor. when you're 18, your world is spinning, spinning, spinning. everything is too loud. too bright. you feel you're at a climax. you're a danger to yourself. a danger to others. you feel reckless and harried. time is running out, yet it is stretching longer and longer out before you. you tell your counselor all of this. you're pacing and your breathing is slightly off. you can't quite hear what you're saying, only that your counselor looks worried and tells you to sit. you try to, but you're too worked up. before you know it, your mom is there to pick you up and leave. you don't know why, but you begin to cry. you can feel it in you. death calling for you and you can't tell it to go away. you'll never forget the way your mother looked at you in the car before she pulled out of the parking lot. when you're 18, you realize no one knows what to do with you.

CRASH CRASH PUTTER PUTTER

the wall
        i'll crash my car into
is a residential wall on a main road.

there is a house behind it.
        other people have crashed into it.
i know it's probably a bad plan.
death   isn't   guaranteed.

if i end up in the   hospital
        i wouldn't be   mad. at least then
the   physical pain will match the   emotional   pain.

it   will be the last thing i do.
        crash my red car into   a wall
my mother will mourn   but i won't be here.

everyone   will wonder what went wrong.
        oblivious   to the pain of others.
my   going away won't even make them
        more aware before the   next time.

IF OTHER PEOPLE DON'T NEED A BRAIN NEITHER DO I

head exploding, landing on all sides of me
i pick it up and put it in a plastic bag
save it for later
i'll need it again
dazedly make my way back home
take the bag and put it in the freezer
it's a problem for tomorrow
lay my body on my bed that's been made
just for me
by me
and rest

IT'S NOT MY BIRTHDAY CAN I CRY ANYWAY?

i'm crying tears
they are big and burning
melting my face
taking my skin off
washing it away
i don't even need to scrub
or claw

they fall down my cheeks
caress the end of my chin
and slip down my neck
i feel hollow, carved out
with a hunting knife
like i am the animal that's hunted for prize

i will be made new when the tears stop flowing
i have nothing inside me
my face will be new
i can be anything, anything at all

YOU'RE THE WORST THING THAT EVER HAPPENED TO ME

i still think of you
it drives me to drink
when a certain smell wrecks through my nose
i crinkle it and wish to smell dog shit
a line in a movie you would quote
i turn it off with a quickness that can only possess
you haunt me and i hate it
from the bottom of my heart i hate that i loved you ever in my
life

YOU KNOW WHAT I MEAN RIGHT?

i do not know who i am
i do not know what i am doing
i feel hopeless trying to be hopeful
pleading that someday i'll make it exactly where i need to be

EVERYTHING IS BREAKING INCLUDING ME

i scream so loud and so high i break the windows, shatter the mirrors, and pierce the glasses. everything around me shatters into a million pieces. my mother comes running, yelling what happened? i stand in the mess i've made and look at her. she walks on broken glass, tip toeing. coming towards me. i stand there, tears streaming down my face. hot and wet and uncomfortable tears. all the fight has left my body. i look around at the destruction i've caused. the mess i've made to get someone to notice me.i fall to my knees. they immediately start to bleed on the glass. i look down through my tears to my arms, and find shards of glass stuck, blood trickling down. i raise my hands and run them down my face, feeling hot blood oozing. i am the mess you've made.